Ketoge...

© *Maya Lyon*

Table of Contents

Introduction

Ketogenic Diet
Mysterious machine
Ketogenic health
Cancer be gone

Recipes

Tartar Keto Cookies
Wild Strawberries Ice Cream
Mini Lemon Cheesecakes
Chocolate Layered Coconut Cups
Pumpkin Pie Chocolate Cups
Fudgy Slow Cooker Cake
Easy Sticky Chocolate Fudge
Raspberry & Coconut Fat Bombs
Strawberry Cheesecake Ice Cream Cups
Peppermint Patties
Buttery Pecan Delights
Fudge Oh So Chocolate
Cinna-Bun Balls
Vanilla Mousse Cups
Rich & Creamy Fat Bomb Ice Cream
English Toffee Treats
Fudgy Peanut Butter Squares

Conclusion

Introduction

I prefer to regard a dessert as I would imagine the perfect woman: subtle, a little bittersweet, not blowsy and extrovert. Delicately made up, not highly rouged. Holding back, not exposing everything and, of course, with a flavor that lasts.

~Graham Kerr

Ketogenic Diet

"My sugar", "my honey", "my candy" – we use these words when referring to our loved ones without even thinking about the deeper meaning hidden beneath these expressions. We love the sweet taste of things and we tend to see it as something desirable but there is a solid body of circumstantial evidence that sugar and sweets - of the dietary kind - might actually be harming us.

As soon as our ancestors grasped the concept of illnesses, they tried to alleviate them through diets of various sorts. Sometimes bizarre and often nothing more than mere guesswork, these diets presumed the existence of mysterious "fluids" in the body that somehow control all physiological processes and associated certain food types with each fluid. However, one such group of diets did involve removing all starch and sweets from the diet. Whether they knew it or not, our ancestors might have been onto something.

Mysterious machine

Today, we know slightly more than our ancestors did about the underlying mechanism that helps our digestive system turn the food we eat into energy that's usable for our cells. Still, the human body is a wonderfully complex biological machine that cannot be accurately replicated inside a controlled scientific environment. This hinders nutritional scientists, who have to test out their theories on the most extreme cases of health issues that do not respond to any medication. Among these medical conditions that drastically influence the quality of life is epilepsy.

There are currently around 50 million people worldwide who suffer from varying degrees of epilepsy. This debilitating medical condition can leave the afflicted completely incapable of normally functioning and has causes which the medical science can't quite articulate. 20% of those who suffer from it do not respond at all to any medication. But, adopting ketogenic diet might do the trick for them.

Ketogenic health

Normally, the body will try to convert carbohydrates ingested through food into glucose that's readily available in blood as fuel for its daily needs. To regulate the amount of glucose in blood, the body constantly drips a hormone known as insulin into the bloodstream. Though this is a natural process that occurs constantly throughout our lives, it appears there is also a number of disorders and ailments connected to it, among which is epilepsy. The so-called ketogenic diet focuses on the fact that the body can and will adapt to the lack of carbohydrates by learning to use a different source of fuel, causing a state known as ketosis.

Ketosis indicates that the body has started to break down its fat reserves and is actively adapting to the new diet. Ketosis can be measured by dipping specialized strips into urine, thus tracking the overall progress of the ketogenic diet. Though it's still unknown how ketosis actually helps the body, extensive studies done on both humans and animals suggest that ketogenic diet helps lessen the incidence and severity of not only epilepsy but a wide array of chronic neurological disorders, such as Alzheimer's and Parkinson's disease. Unlike medication, ketogenic diet also has a protective effect which persists even after the diet is discontinued.

Cancer be gone

Another interesting finding related to the ketogenic diet is that it seems to neutralize cancers before they've even had the chance to take hold in the body. Namely, the tumor uses the overabundance of glucose in the blood to fuel its unstoppable growth and metastasis. But when the main source of energy in the body are ketones, the cancer cells are unable to adapt and grow in this new environment. Again, there appears to be no need to have a lifetime ketogenic diet – even short durations on ketogenic diet seem to have this immunizing effect.

The foods that are used in a ketogenic diet are generally dark-green vegetables, such as lettuce, spinach, kale and green beans. Any starchy or sweet foods (including fruit) should be avoided, with the preferred protein source being poultry. Any food rich in fat, such as butter or bacon, ought to be consumed on a daily basis. The ideal daily intake of carbohydrates is anything below 20 grams per day.

Recipes

All-stars Peanut-Butter Cookies

Ingredients

2 cups peanut butter

1/4 cup Erythritol

2 eggs

1 1/4 cups coconut flour

2 tsp baking soda

2 tsp peanut extract

1/2 tsp kosher salt

Procedure

1. Preheat oven to 345° F.

2. In a bowl beat the peanut butter, coconut flour and Erythritol with an electric mixer (MEDIUM speed) until fluffy. Reduce speed to LOW and add in the eggs, baking soda, vanilla, and salt.

3. With your hands make balls from the batter and place on parchment-lined baking pan. Bake 10 to 15 minutes. When ready, cool slightly and then move from the stove to cool completely. Ready. Serve.

Servings: 18

Cooking Times

Total Time: 1 hour and 15 minutes

Nutrition Facts

Serving size: 1/18 of a recipe (1,4 ounces).

Percent daily values based on the Reference Daily Intake (RDI) for a 2000 calorie diet.

Nutrition information calculated from recipe ingredients. One of the recipe's ingredients was not linked. This ingredient is not included in the recipe nutrition data.

Amount Per Serving

Calories 182,5

Calories From Fat (67%) 123,03

% Daily Value

Total Fat 14,67g 23%

Saturated Fat 4,38g 22%

Cholesterol 20,67mg 7%

Sodium 313,76mg 13%

Potassium 189,65mg 5%

Total Carbohydrates 8,65g 3%

Fiber 1,96g 8%

Sugar 5,58g

Protein 7g 14%

Almond Chocolate Brownies

Ingredients

3 eggs

4 oz dark chocolate, unsweetened

1/2 cup coconut oil

1 cup almond flour

1 cup walnuts

2 Tbs cocoa, unsweetened

1 tsp vanilla essence

2 cups granulated sweetener Stevia or Erythritol

1 tsp baking soda

pinch of salt

Procedure

1. Preheat the oven to 350F.

2. In a container, add almond flour, sweetener, cocoa, salt and baking soda. With an electric mixer, blend the ingredients on the slowest setting until combined well.

3. Melt the chocolate and the coconut oil together (In a microwave or double boiler). Stir thoroughly.

4. Add eggs and vanilla essence to the flour and mix on a medium speed until a thick batter is formed.

5. Add the butter/chocolate mix to the batter continuing on medium speed until an even texture is formed. Line a slice tin or square baking tin with wax paper. Fold in walnut pieces then turn the batter into your slice tin.

6. Bake for 25 minutes. When ready let cool on wire rack.

7. Cut into 16 Brownies and serve.

Servings: 16

Cooking Times

Total Time: 35 minutes

Nutrition Facts

Serving size: 1/16 of a recipe (1,4 ounces).

Percent daily values based on the Reference Daily Intake (RDI) for a 2000 calorie diet.

Nutrition information calculated from recipe ingredients. 3 of the recipe's ingredients were not linked. These ingredients are not included in the recipe nutrition data.

Amount Per Serving

Calories 207,88

Calories From Fat (84%) 175,63

% Daily Value

Total Fat 20,72g 32%

Saturated Fat 9,3g 47%

Cholesterol 34,88mg 12%

Sodium 94,2mg 4%

Potassium 174,98mg 5%

Total Carbohydrates 5,38g 2%

Fiber 2,82g 11%

Sugar 0,73g

Protein 5,14g 10%

Almond Chocolate Cookies

Ingredients

2 cups almond meal

1 1/2 tsp almond extract

4 Tbsp cocoa powder

5 Tbsp coconut oil, melted

2 Tbsp almond milk

4 Tbsp agave nectar

2 tsp vanilla extract

1/8 tsp baking soda

1/8 tsp salt

Procedure

1. Preheat oven to 340F degrees.

2. In a deep bowl mix salt, cocoa powder, almond meal and baking soda.

3. In a separate bowl, whisk together melted coconut oil, almond milk, almond and vanilla extract and maple syrup. Merge the almond meal mixture with almond milk mixture and mix well.

4. In a greased baking pan pour the batter evenly. Bake for 10-15 minutes. 5. Once ready let cool on a wire rack and serve.

Servings: 12

Cooking Times

Total Time: 25 minutes

Nutrition Facts

Serving size: 1/12 of a recipe (3,6 ounces).

Percent daily values based on the Reference Daily Intake (RDI) for a 2000 calorie diet.

Nutrition information calculated from recipe ingredients.

Amount Per Serving

Calories 79,32

Calories From Fat (67%) 53,17

% Daily Value

Total Fat 5,94g 9%

Saturated Fat 5,48g 27%

Cholesterol 0,2mg <1%

Sodium 39,65mg 2%

Potassium 35,78mg 1%

Total Carbohydrates 7,02g 2%

Fiber 0,61g 2%

Sugar 6g

Protein 0,46g <1%

Carrot Flowers Muffins

Ingredients

2 eggs

2 cups shredded carrots

1/4 cup coconut flour

1/2 cup coconut oil

1 tsp vanilla extract

1/4 cup Erythritol

2 tsp ground cinnamon

1 tsp baking powder

Procedure

1. Preheat oven to 350F. Prepare12 muffin tins.

2. In your food processor, add in carrots, eggs, coconut oil, Erythritol, and vanilla. Blend together until combined.

3. In a separate bowl, mix together coconut flour, cinnamon and baking powder.

4. Pour the carrot mixture into the dry ingredients and mix until completely combined.

5. Pour carrot mixture into the muffin tin and bake for about 30-35 minutes.

6. Remove from the oven, and let cool for at least 30 minutes. Serve.

Servings: 12

Cooking Times

Total Time: 50 minutes

Nutrition Facts

Serving size: 1/12 of a recipe (1,7 ounces).

Percent daily values based on the Reference Daily Intake (RDI) for a 2000 calorie diet.

Nutrition information calculated from recipe ingredients.

Amount Per Serving

Calories 127,55

Calories From Fat (68%) 86,89

% Daily Value

Total Fat 10,04g 15%

Saturated Fat 8,14g 41%

Cholesterol 31mg 10%

Sodium 68,15mg 3%

Potassium 101,69mg 3%

Total Carbohydrates 8,81g 3%

Fiber 0,91g 4%

Sugar 5,1g

Protein 1,53g 3%

Coconut Jelly Cake

Ingredients

1 cup coconut flour

1/2 cup butter, softened

2 Tbs raspberry jelly

1/2 cup coconut sugar

3 cups desiccated coconut

1 egg

2/3 cup coconut milk

1 cup boiling water

1 cup cold water

1/2 cup double thick cream

Procedure

1. Preheat oven to 360F. Grease a patty pan.

2. In a bowl beat butter and coconut sugar until light. Add in egg and beat until well combined. Gently fold in half the coconut flour and half the milk. Repeat with remaining flour and milk.

3. Spoon mixture into patty pan. Bake for 15 to 20 minutes. Once ready, let cool cakes on a wire rack.

4. Stir jelly and boiling water together in a bowl until crystals are dissolved. Stir in cold water. Refrigerate for 1 hour.

5. Place coconut into a large bowl. Cut each cake in half. Stick halves back together using 1 teaspoon of cream. Using a slotted spoon lower cakes, 1 cake at a time, into jelly. Drain excess jelly.

6.Toss cakes in coconut until well coated. When ready, place onto a lined tray and refrigerate at least 1 hour or until set.

Servings: 18

Cooking Times

Total Time: 30 minutes

Nutrition Facts

Serving size: 1/18 of a recipe (2,7 ounces).

Percent daily values based on the Reference Daily Intake (RDI) for a 2000 calorie diet.

Nutrition information calculated from recipe ingredients. One of the recipe's ingredients was not linked. This ingredient is not included in the recipe nutrition data.

Amount Per Serving

Calories 146,51

Calories From Fat (84%) 122,51

% Daily Value

Total Fat 14,31g 22%

Saturated Fat 10,98g 55%

Cholesterol 27,24mg 9%

Sodium 30,99mg 1%

Potassium 128,52mg 4%

Total Carbohydrates 4,21g 1%

Fiber 2,16g 9%

Sugar 1,79g

Protein 1,83g 4%

Cottage Pumpkin Pie Ice Cream

Ingredients

1/2 cup toasted pecans, chopped

3 egg yolks

2 Tbsp butter, salted

2 cups coconut milk

1/2 cup pumpkin puree

1 tsp pumpkin spice

1/2 cup cottage cheese

1/2 tsp chia seeds

1/3 cup Erythritol

20 drops liquid Nutria

Procedure

1. Place all ingredients into a container of your immersion blender. Blend all of the ingredients together into a smooth mixture.

2. Add mixture to your ice cream machine, as per instructions of your manufacturer.

3. Follow the churning instructions as per your ice cream maker manufacturer's instructions. Serve in a chilled bowls or glasses.

Servings: 6

Cooking Times

Total Time: 15 minutes

.

Nutrition Facts

Serving size: 1/6 of a recipe (3,6 ounces).

Percent daily values based on the Reference Daily Intake (RDI) for a 2000 calorie diet.

Nutrition information calculated from recipe ingredients. 2 of the recipe's ingredients were not linked. These ingredients are not included in the recipe nutrition data.

Amount Per Serving

Calories 233,69

Calories From Fat (79%) 185,22

% Daily Value

Total Fat 21,74g 33%

Saturated Fat 10,26g 51%

Cholesterol 96,05mg 32%

Sodium 121,82mg 5%

Potassium 202,46mg 6%

Total Carbohydrates 6,87g 2%

Fiber 1,95g 8%

Sugar 1,79g

Protein 5,49g 11%

Divine Keto Chocolate Biscotti

Ingredients

1 egg

2 cups whole almonds

2 Tbs flax seeds

1 cup shredded coconut, unsweetened

1 cup coconut oil

1 cup cacao powder

1/4 cup Xilitol or Stevia sweetener

1 tsp salt

1 tsp baking soda

Procedure

1. Preheat oven to 350F.

2. In a food process blend the whole almonds with the flax seeds. Add in the rest of ingredients and mix well.

3. Place the dough on a piece of aluminum foil to shape into 8 biscotti-shaped slices. Bake for 12 minutes.

4. Let cool and serve.

Servings: 8

Cooking Times

Total Time: 25 minutes

Nutrition Facts

Serving size: 1/8 of a recipe (1,8 ounces).

Percent daily values based on the Reference Daily Intake (RDI) for a 2000 calorie diet.

Nutrition information calculated from recipe ingredients. One of the recipe's ingredients was not linked. This ingredient is not included in the recipe nutrition data.

Amount Per Serving

Calories 276,56

Calories From Fat (78%) 215,02

% Daily Value

Total Fat 25,44g 39%

Saturated Fat 8,36g 42%

Cholesterol 23,25mg 8%

Sodium 241,73mg 10%

Potassium 295,78mg 8%

Total Carbohydrates 9,19g 3%

Fiber 5,2g 21%

Sugar 1,75g

Protein 8,24g 16%

Halloween Pumpkin Ice Cream

Ingredients

1 cup almond milk (unsweetened)

1 cup coconut milk

1 cup pumpkin puree

2 1/2 tsp ground cinnamon

1 tsp pure vanilla extract

1/2 tsp ground ginger

1/2 tsp nutmeg

1/8 tsp sea salt

Thickener:

1/2 tsp guar gum or 1 tablespoon gelatin dissolved in 1/4 cup boiling water

Procedure

1. Put the coconut milk in a blender and purée until smooth.

2. Pour into the ice cream machine or blender and churn well. Serve in chilled glasses.

3. Freeze for about an hour or refrigerate until cold.

4. Add the almond milk, pumpkin puree, vanilla, cinnamon, ginger, nutmeg and salt, plus thickener. Purée until smooth.

5. Serve.

Servings: 6

Cooking Times

Inactive Time: 1 hour

Total Time: 15 minutes

Nutrition Facts

Serving size: 1/6 of a recipe (2,5 ounces).

Percent daily values based on the Reference Daily Intake (RDI) for a 2000 calorie diet.

Nutrition information calculated from recipe ingredients. One of the recipe's ingredients was not linked. This ingredient is not included in the recipe nutrition data.

Amount Per Serving

Calories 118,25

Calories From Fat (80%) 94,63

% Daily Value

Total Fat 11,3g 17%

Saturated Fat 9,97g 50%

Cholesterol 0mg 0%

Sodium 463,03mg 19%

Potassium 193,11mg 6%

Total Carbohydrates 4,73g 2%

Fiber 1,4g 6%

Sugar 1,43g

Protein 1,35g 3%

Hemp and Chia Seeds Cream

Ingredients

1 ¼ cup coconut milk

2 Tbsp hemp powder

2 sheets of unflavored gelatin

3 Tbsp chia seeds

Procedure

1. In a saucepan over low heat add the coconut milk and dissolve the lucuma powder.
2. Cut the gelatin into pieces and add it to the milk. Stir until dissolved completely.
3. Add chia seeds and stir occasionally until mixture thickens, about 15 minutes. Pour the mixture into individual containers and allow cool before putting them in the refrigerator for at least 2 hours before serving. Enjoy!

Servings: 3

Cooking Times

Total Time: 20 minutes

Nutrition Facts

Serving size: 1/3 of a recipe (3,1 ounces).

Percent daily values based on the Reference Daily Intake (RDI) for a 2000 calorie diet.

Nutrition information calculated from recipe ingredients. 2 of the recipe's ingredients were not linked. These ingredients are not included in the recipe nutrition data.

Amount Per Serving

Calories 202,43

Calories From Fat (79%) 160,45

% Daily Value

Total Fat 19,2g 30%

Saturated Fat 15,02g 75%

Cholesterol 0mg 0%

Sodium 11,18mg <1%

Potassium 198,93mg 6%

Total Carbohydrates 8,12g 3%

Fiber 3,14g 13%

Protein 2,59g 5%

Homemade Nuts Bars

Ingredients

1 cup almonds

1/2 cup hazelnut, chopped

1 cup peanuts

1 cup shredded coconut

1 cup almond butter

1 cup Liquid Erythritol

1 cup coconut oil, freshly melted and still warm

Procedure

1. In a food processor place all nuts and chop for 1-2 minutes.

2. Add in grated coconut, almond butter, Erythritol and coconut oil. Process it for 1 minute about.

3. Cover a square bowl with parchment paper and place the mixture on top.

4. Flatten the mixture with a spatula. Place the bowl in the freezer for 4-5 hours.

5. Remove batter from the freezer, cut and serve.

Servings: 10

Cooking Times

Cooking Time: 10 minutes

Inactive Time: 5 hours

Nutrition Facts

Serving size: 1/10 of a recipe (1,3 ounces).

Percent daily values based on the Reference Daily Intake (RDI) for a 2000 calorie diet.

Nutrition information calculated from recipe ingredients.

Amount Per Serving

Calories 193,62

Calories From Fat (79%) 153,66

% Daily Value

Total Fat 18,2g 28%

Saturated Fat 6,86g 34%

Cholesterol 0mg 0%

Sodium 25,94mg 1%

Potassium 146,46mg 4%

Total Carbohydrates 6,64g 2%

Fiber 2,53g 10%

Sugar 2,97g

Protein 3,83g 8%

Keto Avocado Smoothie

Ingredients

1 Haas avocado

3 oz almond milk, unsweetened

3 oz heavy whipping cream

6 drops Liquid Stevia

Ice cubes

Procedure

1. Cut the avocado in half, remove the seed and remove the flesh from the skin.
2. In a blender mix the almond milk, avocado, heavy whipping cream, sweetener and ice cubes. Blend 1 minute.
3. Serve.

Servings: 3

Cooking Times

Total Time: 7 minutes

Nutrition Facts

Serving size: 1/3 of a recipe (3,7 ounces).

Percent daily values based on the Reference Daily Intake (RDI) for a 2000 calorie diet.

Nutrition information calculated from recipe ingredients. 2 of the recipe's ingredients were not linked. These ingredients are not included in the recipe nutrition data.

Amount Per Serving

Calories 252,92

Calories From Fat (83%) 208,84

% Daily Value

Total Fat 24,43g 38%

Saturated Fat 8,26g 41%

Cholesterol 38,84mg 13%

Sodium 15,55mg <1%

Potassium 404,96mg 12%

Total Carbohydrates 8,31g 3%

Fiber 5,51g 22%

Sugar 0,8g

Protein 3,69g 7%

Keto Caramel Coffee Smoothie

Ingredients

1/2 cup heavy cream

1/2 cup almond milk, unsweetened

3 Tbsp sugar-free chocolate syrup

3 Tbsp sugar-free caramel syrup

3/4 cup cold coffee

2 Tbs cocoa, unsweetened

Ice cubes

Procedure

1. In a blender add all ingredients and blend until all incorporate well.
2. Pour in glasses and serve.

Servings: 4

Cooking Times

Total Time: 5 minutes

Nutrition Facts

Serving size: 1/4 of a recipe (1,7 ounces).

Percent daily values based on the Reference Daily Intake (RDI) for a 2000 calorie diet.

Nutrition information calculated from recipe ingredients. 2 of the recipe's ingredients were not linked. These ingredients are not included in the recipe nutrition data.

Amount Per Serving

Calories 170,62

Calories From Fat (76%) 129,87

% Daily Value

Total Fat 14,95g 23%

Saturated Fat 7,36g 37%

Cholesterol 40,79mg 14%

Sodium 26,06mg 1%

Potassium 126,8mg 4%

Total Carbohydrates 9,02g 3%

Fiber 1,92g 8%

Sugar 2,69g

Protein 2,8g 6%

Keto Chia Seeds Cream

Ingredients

1/4 cup Chia seeds

1 cup heavy whipping cream

1 cup coconut milk

2 Tbs cocoa powder

pure vanilla extract

1/4 cup Erythritol sweetener

Procedure

1. In a bowl mix the chia seeds and add the coconut milk until it combines well.

2. Add the Erythritol and whisk some more. Divide the mixture into two portions.

3. Add cocoa to one half and mixed it nicely.

4. Pour chia seed mixture into the bowls or glasses. Keep covered in the refrigerator for 12 hours.

Before serving beat the heavy whipping cream and pour over the chia seeds cream. Enjoy!

Servings: 4

Cooking Times

Total Time: 12 hours

Nutrition Facts

Serving size: 1/4 of a recipe (4,4 ounces).

Percent daily values based on the Reference Daily Intake (RDI) for a 2000 calorie diet.

Nutrition information calculated from recipe ingredients. 2 of the recipe's ingredients were not linked. These ingredients are not included in the recipe nutrition data.

Amount Per Serving

Calories 341,31

Calories From Fat (90%) 305,55

% Daily Value

Total Fat 35,41g 54%

Saturated Fat 25,05g 125%

Cholesterol 81,52mg 27%

Sodium 30,71mg 1%

Potassium 227,81mg 7%

Total Carbohydrates 7,35g 2%

Fiber 1,56g 6%

Sugar 0,11g

Protein 2,99g 6%

KETO Chocolate Brownies

Ingredients

2 eggs

1 1/2 cups almond flour

1/4 cup coconut oil

1/2 cup cocoa powder, unsweetened

1 Tbs Metamucil Fiber Powder

1/3 cup Natvia (or some other natural sweetener)l

1/4 cup maple syrup

1 tsp baking powder

1/2 tsp salt

Procedure

1. Preheat oven to 350F.

2. In a bowl add in all wet ingredients and 2 Eggs. Beat the wet ingredients together using a hand mixer until a consistent mixture is formed.

3. In a separate bowl, combine all dry ingredients. Mix the dry ingredients well. Pour the wet ingredients slowly into the dry ingredients, mixing with a hand mixer as you pour.

4. Pour the batter into baking pan. Bake the brownies for 20 minutes.

5. When ready, let the brownies cool. Slice brownies into slices and serve.

Servings: 10

Cooking Times

Total Time: 35 minutes

Nutrition Facts

Serving size: 1/10 of a recipe (1,3 ounces).

Percent daily values based on the Reference Daily Intake (RDI) for a 2000 calorie diet.

Nutrition information calculated from recipe ingredients. 2 of the recipe's ingredients were not linked. These ingredients are not included in the recipe nutrition data.

Amount Per Serving

Calories 157,81

Calories From Fat (72%) 113,89

% Daily Value

Total Fat 13,4g 21%

Saturated Fat 4,94g 25%

Cholesterol 37,2mg 12%

Sodium 183,28mg 8%

Potassium 171,91mg 5%

Total Carbohydrates 8,07g 3%

Fiber 2,58g 10%

Sugar 3,62g

Protein 5,04g 10%

Keto Chocolate Pecan Bites

Ingredients

2 oz 100% dark chocolate

2.5 oz pecan halves

cinnamon

nutmeg

Procedure

1. Preheat oven to 350F.

2. Place the pecan halves on a parchment paper and bake in oven for 6-7 minutes. When ready, let cool and set aside.

3. Melt the dark chocolate.

4. Dip each pecan half in the melted dark chocolate and place back on the parchment paper.

5. Sprinkle a cinnamon and nutmeg on top of the chocolate covered pecans.

6. Before serving place in refrigerator for 2-3 hours.

Servings: 12

Cooking Times

Total Time: 3 hours

Nutrition Facts

Serving size: 1/12 of a recipe (0,3 ounces).

Percent daily values based on the Reference Daily Intake (RDI) for a 2000 calorie diet.

Nutrition information calculated from recipe ingredients. 2 of the recipe's ingredients were not linked. These ingredients are not included in the recipe nutrition data.

Amount Per Serving

Calories 52,13

Calories From Fat (79%) 41,25

% Daily Value

Total Fat 4,96g 8%

Saturated Fat 0,78g 4%

Cholesterol 0mg 0%

Sodium 0,26mg <1%

Potassium 24,22mg <1%

Total Carbohydrates 2,32g <1%

Fiber 0,71g 3%

Sugar 0,23g

Protein 0,64g 1%

Keto Hazelnuts Chocolate Cream

Ingredients

1 cup hazelnuts halves

4 Tbsp unsweetened cocoa powder

1 tsp pure vanilla extract

2 Tbsp coconut oil

4 Tbsp granulated Stevia (or sweetener of choice)

Procedure

1. Place all the ingredients in your blender. Blend until smooth well.

2. Store in the fridge for 1 hour. Serve and enjoy!

Servings: 4

Cooking Times

Total Time: 5 minutes

Nutrition Facts

Serving size: 1/4 of a recipe (1,7 ounces).

Percent daily values based on the Reference Daily Intake (RDI) for a 2000 calorie diet.

Nutrition information calculated from recipe ingredients. One of the recipe's ingredients was not linked. This ingredient is not included in the recipe nutrition data.

Amount Per Serving

Calories 302,88

Calories From Fat (83%) 249,89

% Daily Value

Total Fat 29,65g 46%

Saturated Fat 7,92g 40%

Cholesterol 0mg 0%

Sodium 1,23mg <1%

Potassium 351,4mg 10%

Total Carbohydrates 9,5g 3%

Fiber 5,12g 20%

Sugar 1,96g

Protein 6,39g 13%

Keto Instant Coffee Ice Cream

Ingredients

1 Tbsp Instant Coffee

2 Tbsp Cocoa Powder

1 cup coconut milk

1/4 cup heavy cream

1/4 tsp flax seeds

2 Tbs Erythritol

15 drops liquid Nutria

Procedure

1. Add all ingredients except the flax seeds into a container of your immersion blender.
2. Blend well until all ingredients are incorporated well. Slowly add in flax seeds until a slightly thicker mixture is formed. Add the mass to your ice cream machine and follow manufacturer's instructions.
3. Ready! Serve!

Servings: 2

Cooking Times

Total Time: 20 minutes

Nutrition Facts

Serving size: 1/2 of a recipe (4,4 ounces).

Percent daily values based on the Reference Daily Intake (RDI) for a 2000 calorie diet.

Nutrition information calculated from recipe ingredients. 2 of the recipe's ingredients were not linked. These ingredients are not included in the recipe nutrition data.

Amount Per Serving

Calories 286,99

Calories From Fat (86%) 247,72

% Daily Value

Total Fat 29,21g 45%

Saturated Fat 23,36g 117%

Cholesterol 30,98mg 10%

Sodium 21,51mg <1%

Potassium 340,42mg 10%

Total Carbohydrates 9,39g 3%

Fiber 1,88g 8%

Sugar 0,12g

Protein 3,18g 6%

Keto Jam "Eye" Cookies

Ingredients

2 eggs

1 cup almond flour

2 Tbsp coconut flour

2 Tbsp sugar-free jam per taste

1/2 cup natural sweetener (Stevia, Truvia, Erythritol...etc.)

4 Tbs coconut oil

1/2 tsp pure vanilla extract

1/2 tsp almond extract

1 Tbs shredded coconut

1/2 tsp baking powder

1/4 tsp cinnamon

1/2 tsp salt

Procedure

1. Preheat your oven to 350F. In a big bowl, combine all your dry ingredients and whisk.

2. Add in your wet ingredients and combine well using hand mixer or a whisk.

3. With your hand for make the patties and place the cookies on a parchment paper lined baking sheet. Using your finger make an indent in the middle if each cookie.

4. Bake for about 16 minutes or until the cookies turn golden.

5. Once ready, let the cookies cool on a wire rack and fill each indent with sugar free jam.

6. Before serving sprinkle some shredded coconut on top of each cookie. Enjoy!

Servings: 16

Cooking Times

Total Time: 36 minutes

Nutrition Facts

Serving size: 1/16 of a recipe (0,7 ounces).

Percent daily values based on the Reference Daily Intake (RDI) for a 2000 calorie diet.

Nutrition information calculated from recipe ingredients. 2 of the recipe's ingredients were not linked. These ingredients are not included in the recipe nutrition data.

Amount Per Serving

Calories 95,1

Calories From Fat (77%) 73,47

% Daily Value

Total Fat 8,61g 13%

Saturated Fat 3,57g 18%

Cholesterol 23,25mg 8%

Sodium 97,92mg 4%

Potassium 73,57mg 2%

Total Carbohydrates 2,79g <1%

Fiber 1,02g 4%

Sugar 0,59g

Protein 2,71g 5%

Keto Lemon Coconut Pearls

Ingredients

3 packages of True Lemon (Crystallized Citrus for Water)

1/4 cup shredded coconut, unsweetened

1 cup cream cheese

1/4 cup granulated Stevia

Procedure

1. In a bowl, combine cream cheese, lemon and Stevia. Blend well until incorporate.

2. Once the mixture is well combined, put it back in the fridge to harden up a bit.

3. Roll into 16 balls and dip each ball into shredded coconut. Refrigerate for several hours. Serve.

Servings: 4

Cooking Times

Total Time: 15 minutes

Nutrition Facts

Serving size: 1/4 of a recipe (2,2 ounces).

Percent daily values based on the Reference Daily Intake (RDI) for a 2000 calorie diet.

Nutrition information calculated from recipe ingredients. 2 of the recipe's ingredients were not linked. These ingredients are not included in the recipe nutrition data.

Amount Per Serving

Calories 216,06

Calories From Fat (87%) 188,56

% Daily Value

Total Fat 21,53g 33%

Saturated Fat 12,67g 63%

Cholesterol 63,8mg 21%

Sodium 187,18mg 8%

Potassium 97,84mg 3%

Total Carbohydrates 3,12g 1%

Fiber 0,45g 2%

Sugar 2,17g

Protein 3,61g 7%

Keto Lime Cheesecake

Ingredients

1/4 cup cream cheese, softened

2 Tbsp heavy cream

1 tsp lime juice

1 egg

1 tsp pure vanilla extract

2-4 Tbsp Eerythritol or Stevia

Procedure

1. In a microwave-safe bowl combine all ingredients. Place in a microwave and cook on HIGH for 90 seconds.
2. Every 30 seconds stir to combine the ingredients well.
3. Transfer mixture to a bowl and refrigerate for at least 2 hours.
4. Before serving top with whipped cream or coconut powder.

Servings: 2

Cooking Times

Preparation Time: 5 minutes

Inactive Time: 2 hours

Nutrition Facts

Serving size: 1/2 of a recipe (2 ounces).

Percent daily values based on the Reference Daily Intake (RDI) for a 2000 calorie diet.

Nutrition information calculated from recipe ingredients. One of the recipe's ingredients was not linked. This ingredient is not included in the recipe nutrition data.

Amount Per Serving

Calories 140,42

Calories From Fat (82%) 115,18

% Daily Value

Total Fat 13,04g 20%

Saturated Fat 7,12g 36%

Cholesterol 129,96mg 43%

Sodium 89,4mg 4%

Potassium 68,68mg 2%

Total Carbohydrates 1,38g <1%

Fiber 0,01g <1%

Sugar 0,68g

Protein 4,34g 9%

Keto Mouse Chocolate

Ingredients

1/4 cup of heavy cream

1 1/4 cup coconut cream

2 Tbsp of cocoa powder

3 Tbs of Erythritol (or Stevia)

1 Tbsp pure vanilla essence

shredded coconut, unsweetened

Procedure

1. Scoop out the hardened coconut cream from the can, leaving the clear liquid behind, and place into a bowl. Add the heavy cream and combine with a hand mixer on low speed.

2. Add the remaining ingredients and mix on low speed for 2-3 minutes until the mix is thick.

3. Serve in individual ramekins sprinkled with unsweetened shredded coconut.

Servings: 4

Cooking Times

Total Time: 15 minutes

Nutrition Facts

Serving size: 1/4 of a recipe (3,3 ounces).

Percent daily values based on the Reference Daily Intake (RDI) for a 2000 calorie diet.

Nutrition information calculated from recipe ingredients. 3 of the recipe's ingredients were not linked. These ingredients are not included in the recipe nutrition data.

Amount Per Serving

Calories 305,19

Calories From Fat (88%) 269,46

% Daily Value

Total Fat 31,91g 49%

Saturated Fat 26,72g 134%

Cholesterol 20,46mg 7%

Sodium 9,24mg <1%

Potassium 296,1mg 8%

Total Carbohydrates 6,97g 2%

Fiber 2,55g 10%

Sugar 0,06g

Protein 3,56g 7%

Keto Strawberry Pudding

Ingredients

4 egg yolks

2 Tbsp butter

1/4 cup coconut flour

2 Tbsp heavy cream

1/4 cup strawberries

1/4 tsp baking powder

2 Tbsp coconut oil

2 tsp lemon juice

Zest 1 Lemon

2 Tbsp Erythritol

10 drops Liquid Stevia

Procedure

1. Preheat oven to 350F.
2. In a bowl beat the egg yolks with electric mixer until they're pale in color. Add in Erythritol and 10 drops liquid Stevia. Beat again until fully combined.
3. Add in heavy cream, lemon juice, and the zest of 1 lemon. Add the coconut and butter. Beat well until no lumps are found.
4. Sift the dry ingredients over the wet ingredients, then mix well on a slow speed.
5. Distribute the strawberries evenly in the batter by pushing them into the top of the batter.
6. Bake for 20-25 minutes. Once finished, let cool for 5 minutes and serve.

Servings: 3

Cooking Times

Total Time: 35 minutes

Nutrition Facts

Serving size: 1/3 of a recipe (2,3 ounces).

Percent daily values based on the Reference Daily Intake (RDI) for a 2000 calorie diet.

Nutrition information calculated from recipe ingredients. 3 of the recipe's ingredients were not linked. These ingredients are not included in the recipe nutrition data.

Amount Per Serving

Calories 258,65

Calories From Fat (80%) 205,81

% Daily Value

Total Fat 23,46g 36%

Saturated Fat 15,49g 77%

Cholesterol 207,28mg 69%

Sodium 52,09mg 2%

Potassium 69,26mg 2%

Total Carbohydrates 9,3g 3%

Fiber 0,61g 2%

Sugar 0,97g

Protein 3,98g 8%

Kiwi Fiend Ice Cream

Ingredients

3 egg yolks

1 1/2 cup Kiwi, pureed

1 cup heavy cream

1/3 cup Erythritol

1/2 tsp pure vanilla extract

1/8 tsp chia seeds

Procedure

1. In a sauce pan heat up the heavy cream. Add in 1/3 cup of erythritol to dissolve; simmer gently until erythritol is dissolved.

2. In a mixing bowl beat 3 egg yolks with an electric mixer. Add in a few tablespoons of your hot cream mixture at a time to the eggs while beating. Add in some pure vanilla extract and mix. Add in 1/8 tsp. of chia seeds.

3. Place your bowl into the freezer to chill for about 1-2 hours, stirring occasionally.

4. In a meanwhile puree the kiwi no more than 1-2 seconds. When the ice cream is chilled and getting a bit thicker, add in kiwi mixture to the chilled cream. Mix a bit.

5. Let the kiwi ice cream to chill at least 6-8 hours. Serve in chilled glasses.

Servings: 6

Cooking Times

Cooking Time: 15 minutes

Total Time: 8 hours and 15 minutes

Nutrition Facts

Serving size: 1/6 of a recipe (3,3 ounces).

Percent daily values based on the Reference Daily Intake (RDI) for a 2000 calorie diet.

Nutrition information calculated from recipe ingredients. 2 of the recipe's ingredients were not linked. These ingredients are not included in the recipe nutrition data.

Amount Per Serving

Calories 192,47

Calories From Fat (79%) 151,69

% Daily Value

Total Fat 17,2g 26%

Saturated Fat 9,95g 50%

Cholesterol 144,4mg 48%

Sodium 20,46mg <1%

Potassium 179,67mg 5%

Total Carbohydrates 8,13g 3%

Fiber 1,46g 6%

Sugar 4,14g

Protein 2,69g 5%

Minty Avocado Lime Sorbet

Ingredients

1 cup coconut milk

2 avocados

1/4 mint leaves, chopped

1/4 cup powdered Erythritol

2 limes, juiced

1/4 tsp liquid Stevia

Procedure

1. Slice avocado half vertically through the flesh, making about 5 slices per half of an avocado. Use a spoon to carefully scoop out the pieces. Rest pieces on foil and squeeze juice of 1/2 lime over the tops.

2. Store avocado in freezer for at least 3 hours.

3. Using a spice grinder, powder Erythritol.

4. In a pan, bring coconut milk to a boil.

5. Zest the 2 limes you have while coconut milk is heating up. Add lime zest and continue to let the milk reduce in volume.

6. Remove and place the coconut milk into a container and store in the freezer.

7. Chop mint leaves. Remove avocados from freezer.

8. Add avocado, mint leaves, and juice from lime into the food processor. Pulse until a chunky consistency is achieved.

9. Pour coconut milk mixture over the avocados in the food processor. Add Liquid Stevia to this.

10. Pulse mixture together about 2-3 minutes.

11. Return to freezer to freeze, or serve immediately!

Servings: 6

Cooking Times

Total Time: 3 hours and 15 minutes

Nutrition Facts

Serving size: 1/6 of a recipe (4,3 ounces).

Percent daily values based on the Reference Daily Intake (RDI) for a 2000 calorie diet.

Nutrition information calculated from recipe ingredients. 2 of the recipe's ingredients were not linked. These ingredients are not included in the recipe nutrition data.

Amount Per Serving

Calories 184,18

Calories From Fat (78%) 144,45

% Daily Value

Total Fat 17,26g 27%

Saturated Fat 8,61g 43%

Cholesterol 0mg 0%

Sodium 10,03mg <1%

Potassium 410,98mg 12%

Total Carbohydrates 9,65g 3%

Fiber 4,59g 18%

Sugar 0,55g

Protein 1,95g 4%

Morning Zephyr Cake

Ingredients

3 Tbsp coconut oil

2 Tbsp grounded flax seeds

8 Tbsp almonds, grounded

1 cup Greek Yogurt

1 Tbsp cocoa powder for dusting

1 cup heavy whipping cream

1 tsp Baking Powder

1 tsp Baking Soda

1 tsp pure vanilla essence

1 pinch pink salt

1 cup Stevia or Erythritol sweetener

Procedure

1. Pre-heat the oven at 350 F degrees.

2. In the blender first add the grounded almonds, grounded flax seeds and the baking powder and soda. Blend for a minute.

3. Add the salt, coconut oil and blend some more. Add the sweetener and blend for 2-3 minutes.

4. Add the Greek yogurt and blend for a minute or so, until a fine consistency is reached.

5. Take out the batter in a bowl and add the vanilla essence, and mix with a light hand.

6. Grease the baking dish and drop the batter in it.

7. Bake for 30 minutes. Let cool on a wire rack. Serve.

Servings: 8

Cooking Times

Total Time: 40 minutes

Nutrition Facts

Serving size: 1/8 of a recipe (2,3 ounces).

Percent daily values based on the Reference Daily Intake (RDI) for a 2000 calorie diet.

Nutrition information calculated from recipe ingredients. 3 of the recipe's ingredients were not linked. These ingredients are not included in the recipe nutrition data.

Amount Per Serving

Calories 199,84

Calories From Fat (90%) 179,13

% Daily Value

Total Fat 20,69g 32%

Saturated Fat 11,67g 58%

Cholesterol 40,76mg 14%

Sodium 151,45mg 6%

Potassium 94,4mg 3%

Total Carbohydrates 3,22g 1%

Fiber 1,17g 5%

Sugar 0,47g

Protein 2,56g 5%

Peanut Butter Balls

Ingredients

2 eggs

2 1/2 cup of peanut butter

1/2 cup shredded coconut (unsweetened)

1/2 cup of Xylitol

1 Tbsp of pure vanilla extract

Procedure

1. Preheat oven to 320 F.

2. Mix all ingredients together by your hands.

3. After the ingredients are thoroughly mixed, roll into heaped tablespoon sized balls and press into a baking tray lined with baking paper.

4. Bake in the oven for 12 minutes or until the tops of the cookies are browning. When ready, let cool on a wire rack. Ready! Serve.

Servings: 16

Cooking Times

Total Time: 22 minutes

Nutrition Facts

Serving size: 1/16 of a recipe (1,7 ounces).

Percent daily values based on the Reference Daily Intake (RDI) for a 2000 calorie diet.

Nutrition information calculated from recipe ingredients. 2 of the recipe's ingredients were not linked. These ingredients are not included in the recipe nutrition data.

Amount Per Serving

Calories 254,83

Calories From Fat (72%) 182,27

% Daily Value

Total Fat 21,75g 33%

Saturated Fat 5,17g 26%

Cholesterol 23,25mg 8%

Sodium 194,41mg 8%

Potassium 279,15mg 8%

Total Carbohydrates 8,31g 3%

Fiber 2,64g 11%

Sugar 3,9g

Protein 10,98g 22%

Pecan Flax Seed Blondies

Ingredients

3 eggs

2 1/4 cups pecans, roasted

3 Tbs heavy cream

1 Tbs salted caramel syrup

1/2 cup flax seeds, ground

1/4 cup butter, melted

1/4 cup erythritol, powdered

10 drops Liquid Stevia

1 tsp baking powder

1 pinch salt

Procedure

1. Preheat oven to 350F.
2. In a baking pan roast pecans for 10 minutes.
3. Grind 1/2 cup flax seeds in a spice grinder. Place flax seed powder in a bowl. Grind Erythritol in a spice grinder until powdered. Set in the same bowl as the flax seeds meal.
4. Place 2/3 of roasted pecans in food processor and process until a smooth nut butter is formed.
5. Add eggs, liquid Stevia, salted caramel syrup, and a pinch of salt to the flax seed mixture. Mix well. Add pecan butter to the batter and mix again.
6. Smash the rest of the roasted pecans into chunks. Add crushed pecans and 1/4 cup melted butter into the batter.
7. Mix batter well, and then add heavy cream and baking powder. Mix everything together well.
8. Place the batter into baking tray and bake for 20 minute. Let cool for about 10 minutes. Slice off the edges of the brownie to create a uniform square. Serve.

Servings: 16

Cooking Times

Total Time: 40 minutes

Nutrition Facts

Serving size: 1/16 of a recipe (1,5 ounces).

Percent daily values based on the Reference Daily Intake (RDI) for a 2000 calorie diet.

Nutrition information calculated from recipe ingredients. 3 of the recipe's ingredients were not linked. These ingredients are not included in the recipe nutrition data.

Amount Per Serving

Calories 180,45

Calories From Fat (86%) 154,63

% Daily Value

Total Fat 18,23g 28%

Saturated Fat 3,62g 18%

Cholesterol 44,42mg 15%

Sodium 134,77mg 6%

Potassium 109,9mg 3%

Total Carbohydrates 3,54g 1%

Fiber 1,78g 7%

Sugar 1,45g

Protein 3,07g 6%

Peppermint Chocolate Ice Cream

Ingredients

1/2 tsp Peppermint extract

1 cup heavy cream

1 cup cheese cream

1 tsp pure vanilla extract

1 tsp Liquid Stevia extract

100% Dark Chocolate for topping

Procedure

1. Place ice cream bowl in freezer per ice cream maker instructions. In a metal bowl, put all ingredients except chocolate and whisk well.

2. Put back in freezer for 5 minutes. Setup ice cream maker and add liquid.

3. Before serving, top the ice cream with chocolate shavings. Serve.

Servings: 3

Cooking Times

Total Time: 35 minutes

Nutrition Facts

Serving size: 1/3 of a recipe (3 ounces).

Percent daily values based on the Reference Daily Intake (RDI) for a 2000 calorie diet.

Nutrition information calculated from recipe ingredients. One of the recipe's ingredients was not linked. This ingredient is not included in the recipe nutrition data.

Amount Per Serving

Calories 286,66

Calories From Fat (92%) 263,47

% Daily Value

Total Fat 29,96g 46%

Saturated Fat 18,18g 91%

Cholesterol 107,04mg 36%

Sodium 97,15mg 4%

Potassium 77,68mg 2%

Total Carbohydrates 2,7g <1%

Fiber 0g 0%

Sugar 0,9g

Protein 2,6g 5%

Puff-up Coconut Waffles

Ingredients

1 cup coconut flour

1/2 cup heavy (whipping) cream

5 eggs

1/4 tsp pink salt

1/4 tsp baking soda

1/4 cup coconut milk

2 tsp Yacon Syrup (or some other natural sweetener)

2 Tbsp coconut oil (melted)

Procedure

1. In a large bowl add the eggs and beat with an electric hand mixer for 30 seconds.

2. Add the heavy (whipping) cream and coconut oil into the eggs while you are still mixing. Add the coconut milk, coconut flour, pink salt and baking soda. Mix with the hand mixer for 45 second on low speed. Set aside.

3. Heat up your waffle maker well and make the waffles according to your manufactures specifications.

4. Serve hot.

Servings: 8

Nutrition Facts

Serving size: 1/8 of a recipe (2,1 ounces).

Percent daily values based on the Reference Daily Intake (RDI) for a 2000 calorie diet.

Nutrition information calculated from recipe ingredients.

Amount Per Serving

Calories 169,21

Calories From Fat (66%) 111,01

% Daily Value

Total Fat 12,6g 19%

Saturated Fat 8,39g 42%

Cholesterol 97,69mg 33%

Sodium 76,39mg 3%

Potassium 82,99mg 2%

Total Carbohydrates 9,97g 3%

Fiber 0,45g 2%

Sugar 0,38g

Protein 4,39g 9%

Raspberry Chocolate Cream

Ingredients

1/2 cup 100% dark chocolate, chopped

1/4 cup of heavy cream

1/2 cup cream cheese, softened

2 Tbsp sugar free Raspberry Syrup

1/4 cup Erythritol

Procedure

1. In a double boiler melt chopped chocolate and the cream cheese. Add the Erythritol sweetener and continue to stir. Remove from heat, let cool and set aside.

2. When the cream has cooled add in heavy cream and Raspberry syrup and stir well.

3. Pour cream in a bowls or glasses and serve. Keep refrigerated.

Servings: 4

Cooking Times

Total Time: 15 minutes

Nutrition Facts

Serving size: 1/4 of a recipe (1,3 ounces).

Percent daily values based on the Reference Daily Intake (RDI) for a 2000 calorie diet.

Nutrition information calculated from recipe ingredients. One of the recipe's ingredients was not linked. This ingredient is not included in the recipe nutrition data.

Amount Per Serving

Calories 157,67

Calories From Fat (76%) 119,77

% Daily Value

Total Fat 13,51g 21%

Saturated Fat 7,83g 39%

Cholesterol 30,12mg 10%

Sodium 59,94mg 2%

Potassium 100,51mg 3%

Total Carbohydrates 7,47g 2%

Fiber 1g 4%

Sugar 5,16g

Protein 1,95g 4%

Raw Cacao Hazelnut Cookies

Ingredients

2 cups almond flour

1 cup chopped hazelnut

1/2 cup cacao powder

1/2 cup ground flax

3 Tbsp coconut oil (melted)

1/3 cup water

1/3 cup Erythritol

1/4 tsp liquid Stevia

Procedure

1. In a bowl, mix almond flour and flax and cacao powder. Stir in oil, water, agave and vanilla. When it is well mixed, stir in chopped hazelnuts.
2. Form in to balls, press flat with palms and place on dehydrator screens.
3. Dehydrate 1 hour at 145, then reduce to 116 and dehydrate for at least 5 hours or until desired dryness is achieved.
4. Serve.

Servings: 24

Cooking Times

Total Time: 6 hours

Nutrition Facts

Serving size: 1/24 of a recipe (1,3 ounces).

Percent daily values based on the Reference Daily Intake (RDI) for a 2000 calorie diet.

Nutrition information calculated from recipe ingredients.

Amount Per Serving

Calories 181,12

Calories From Fat (73%) 132,76

% Daily Value

Total Fat 15,69g 24%

Saturated Fat 1,51g 8%

Cholesterol 0mg 0%

Sodium 2,38mg <1%

Potassium 205,98mg 6%

Total Carbohydrates 8,75g 3%

Fiber 3,45g 14%

Sugar 3,75g

Protein 4,46g 9%

Sinless Pumpkin Cheesecake Muffins

Ingredients

1/2 cup pureed pumpkin

1 tsp pumpkin pie spice

1/2 cup pecans, finely ground

1/2 cup cream cheese

1 Tbs coconut oil

1/2 tsp pure vanilla extract

1/4 tsp pure Yacon Syrup or Erythritol

Procedure

1. Prepare a muffin tin with liners.

2. Place a small amount of ground pecans into every muffin tin and make a thin crust.

3. In a bowl, blend sweetener, spices, vanilla, coconut and the pumpkin puree. Add in the cream cheese and beat until the mixture is well combined.

4. Scoop about two tablespoons of filling mixture on top of each crust, and smooth around the edges.

5. Pop in the freezer for about 45 minutes.

6. Remove from the muffin tin and let sit for 10 minutes. Serve.

Servings: 6

Cooking Times
Total Time: 15 minutes

Nutrition Facts

Serving size: 1/6 of a recipe (1,8 ounces).

Percent daily values based on the Reference Daily Intake (RDI) for a 2000 calorie diet.

Nutrition information calculated from recipe ingredients. One of the recipe's ingredients was not linked. This ingredient is not included in the recipe nutrition data.

Amount Per Serving

Calories 157,34

Calories From Fat (85%) 133,24

% Daily Value

Total Fat 15,52g 24%

Saturated Fat 6,3g 32%

Cholesterol 21,27mg 7%

Sodium 111,44mg 5%

Potassium 108,38mg 3%

Total Carbohydrates 3,94g 1%

Fiber 1,51g 6%

Sugar 1,72g

Protein 2,22g 4%

Sour Hazelnuts Biscuits with Arrowroot Tea

Ingredients

1 egg

1/2 cup hazelnuts

3 Tbsp of coconut oil

2 cups almond flour

2 Tbsp of arrowroot tea

2 tsp ginger

1 Tbsp cocoa powder

1/2 cup grapefruit juice

1 orange peel from a half orange

1/2 tsp baking soda

1 pinch of salt

Procedure

1. Preheat oven to 360 °F. Make arrowroot tea and let it cool.

2. In a food processor blend the hazelnuts. Add the remaining ingredients and continue blending until mixed well. With your hands form a cookies with the batter.

3. Put the cookies on baking parchment paper, and bake for 30-35 minutes. When ready, remove tray from the oven and let cool.

4. Serve warm or cold.

Servings: 12

Cooking Times

Total Time: 50 minutes

Nutrition Facts

Serving size: 1/12 of a recipe (2 ounces).

Percent daily values based on the Reference Daily Intake (RDI) for a 2000 calorie diet.

Nutrition information calculated from recipe ingredients. One of the recipe's ingredients was not linked. This ingredient is not included in the recipe nutrition data.

Amount Per Serving

Calories 224,08

Calories From Fat (76%) 169,9

% Daily Value

Total Fat 20,17g 31%

Saturated Fat 4,34g 22%

Cholesterol 15,5mg 5%

Sodium 83,49mg 3%

Potassium 262,27mg 7%

Total Carbohydrates 8,06g 3%

Fiber 3,25g 13%

Sugar 2,94g

Protein 6,36g 13%

Tartar Keto Cookies

Ingredients

3 eggs

1/8 tsp cream of tartar

1/3 cup cream cheese

1/8 tsp salt

some oil for greasing

Procedure

1. Preheat oven to 300°F. Line the cookie sheet with parchment paper and grease with some oil.

2. Separate eggs from the egg yolks. Set both in different mixing bowls.

3. With an electric hand mixer, start beating the egg whites until super bubbly. Add in cream of tartar and beat until stiff peaks form.

4. In the egg yolk bowl, add in cream cheese and some salt. Beat until the egg yolks are pale yellow.

5. Merge the egg whites into the cream cheese mixture. Stir well.

6. Make cookies and place on the cookie sheet.

7. Bake for about 30-40 minutes. When ready, let them cool on a wire rack and serve.

Servings: 8

Cooking Times

Total Time: 35 minutes

Nutrition Facts

Serving size: 1/8 of a recipe (1 ounces).

Percent daily values based on the Reference Daily Intake (RDI) for a 2000 calorie diet.

Nutrition information calculated from recipe ingredients. One of the recipe's ingredients was not linked. This ingredient is not included in the recipe nutrition data.

Amount Per Serving

Calories 59,99

Calories From Fat (75%) 45,15

% Daily Value

Total Fat 5,09g 8%

Saturated Fat 2,45g 12%

Cholesterol 80,38mg 27%

Sodium 94,01mg 4%

Potassium 46,96mg 1%

Total Carbohydrates 0,56g <1%

Fiber 0g 0%

Sugar 0,38g

Protein 2,93g 6%

Wild Strawberries Ice Cream

Ingredients

1/2 cup wild strawberries

1/3 cup cream cheese

1 cup heavy cream

1 Tbs lemon juice

1 tsp pure vanilla extract

1/3 cup of your favorite sweetener

Ice cubes

Procedure

1. Place all ingredients in a blender. Blend until all incorporate well.
2. Refrigerate for 2-3 hour before serving.

Servings: 4

Cooking Times

Total Time: 5 minutes

Nutrition Facts

Serving size: 1/4 of a recipe (2,5 ounces).

Percent daily values based on the Reference Daily Intake (RDI) for a 2000 calorie diet.

Nutrition information calculated from recipe ingredients. 2 of the recipe's ingredients were not linked. These ingredients are not included in the recipe nutrition data.

Amount Per Serving

Calories 176,43

Calories From Fat (88%) 155,55

% Daily Value

Total Fat 17,69g 27%

Saturated Fat 10,59g 53%

Cholesterol 62,02mg 21%

Sodium 73,62mg 3%

Potassium 82,38mg 2%

Total Carbohydrates 3,37g 1%

Fiber 0,39g 2%

Sugar 1,71g

Protein 1,9g 4%

Mini Lemon Cheesecakes

INGREDIENTS

1 tablespoon lemon zest, grated

1 teaspoon lemon juice

2 tablespoons sugar substitute

1/4 cup coconut oil, softened

4 tablespoons unsalted butter, softened

4 ounces cream cheese

Instructions:

- Blend all ingredients together with a hand mixer or blender until smooth and creamy.

- Prepare a cupcake or muffin tin with 6 paper liners.

- Pour mixture into prepared tin and place in freezer for 2-3 hours or until firm.

- Sprinkle cups with additional lemon zest. Or try using chopped nuts or shredded, unsweetened coconut.

Serves: 6

Cooking Times

Total Time: 5 minutes

Calories: 196

Fat: 21.2 grams

Chocolate Layered Coconut Cups

INGREDIENTS

Bottom Layer:

1/2 cup unsweetened, shredded coconut

3 tablespoons powdered sweetener such as Splenda or Truvia

1/2 cup coconut butter

1/2 cup coconut oil

Top Layer:

1 1/2 ounces cocoa butter

1 ounce unsweetened chocolate

1/4 cup cocoa powder

1/2 teaspoon vanilla extract

1/4 cup powdered sweetener such as Splenda or Truvia

Instructions:

- Prepare a mini-muffin pan with 20 mini paper liners.

- For the bottom layer:

- Combine coconut butter and coconut oil in a small saucepan over low heat. Stir until smooth and melted then add the shredded coconut and powdered sweetener until combined.

- Divide the mixture among prepared mini muffin cups and freeze until firm, about 30 minutes.

- For the top layer:

- Combine cocoa butter and unsweetened chocolate together in double boiler or a bowl set over a pan of simmering water. Stir until melted.

- Stir in the powdered sweetener, then the cocoa powder and mix until smooth.

- Remove from heat and stir in the vanilla extract.

- Spoon chocolate topping over chilled coconut candies and let set, about 15 minutes.

- Enjoy!

Serves: 10

Serving Size: 2 pieces

Calories: 240

Fat: 25 grams

Pumpkin Pie Chocolate Cups

INGREDIENTS

For the crust:

3.5 ounces extra dark chocolate - 85% cocoa solids or more

2 tablespoons coconut oil

For the pie:

½ cup coconut butter

¼ cup coconut oil

2 teaspoons pumpkin pie spice mix

½ cup unsweetened pumpkin puree

2 tablespoons healthy low-carb sweetener

Optional: 15-20 drops liquid stevia for added sweetness

Instructions:

- Place the chocolate and coconut oil in a double boiler or a glass bowl on top of a small saucepan filled with simmering water. Once completely melted, remove from the heat and set aside.

- Prepare a mini muffin tin with 18 paper liners. Fill each of the 18 mini muffin cups with 2 teaspoons of the chocolate mixture. Place the chocolate in the fridge to set up for at least 10 minutes.

- Place the coconut butter, coconut oil, sweetener and pumpkin spice mix into a bowl and melt just like you did the chocolate.

- Add the pumpkin puree and mix until smooth and well combined.

- Remove the muffin cups from the fridge and add a heaping teaspoon of the pumpkin & coconut mixture into every cup. Place back in the fridge and let it set for at least 30 minutes.

- When done, keep refrigerated. Coconut oil and butter get very soft at room temperature. Store in the fridge for up to a week or freeze for up to 3 months. Enjoy!

Serves: 18

Serving Size: 1 mini pie

Calories: 110

Fat: 10.9 grams

Fudgy Slow Cooker Cake

INGREDIENTS

1 1/2 cups almond flour

1/4 cup whey protein powder (chocolate, vanilla, and unflavored all work fine)

3/4 cup sugar substitute such as Swerve or Truvia

2/3 cup cocoa powder

2 teaspoons baking powder

1/4 teaspoon sea salt

1/2 cup butter, melted

4 large eggs

3/4 cup almond or coconut milk, unsweetened

1 teaspoon vanilla extract

1/2 cup chopped dark chocolate, 85% cocoa or higher

Whipped cream topping (optional):

1/2 cup heavy whipping cream

2 tablespoons sugar substitute

Instructions:

- Grease the insert of a 6 quart slow cooker well with butter or coconut oil.

- In a medium bowl, whisk together almond flour, sugar substitute, cocoa powder, whey protein powder, baking powder and salt.

- Stir in butter, eggs, almond milk and vanilla extract until well combined, then fold in the chopped dark chocolate.

- Pour into the greased slow cooker and cook on low for 2.5 to 3 hours. It will be gooey and like a pudding cake at 2.5 hours, and little more cake like at 3 hours.

- Turn slow cooker off and let cool for 20 to 30 minutes. Cut into pieces and serve warm.

- Best when served with freshly whipped cream. To make this, mix the whipping cream and sugar substitute together with your stand mixer, or a hand mixer. Continue mixing until soft peaks form.

Serves: 10

Serving Size: 1/10th of cake

Calories: 275

Fat: 23

Easy Sticky Chocolate Fudge

INGREDIENTS

1 cup coconut oil, softened

1/4 cup coconut milk (full fat, from a can)

1/4 cup cocoa powder

1 teaspoon vanilla extract

1/2 teaspoon sea salt

1-3 drops liquid stevia

Instructions:

- With a hand mixer or stand mixer, whip the softened coconut oil and coconut milk together until smooth and glossy. About 6 minutes on high.
- Add the cocoa powder, vanilla extract, sea salt, and one drop of liquid stevia to the bowl and mix on low until combined. Increase speed once everything is combined and mix for one minute. Taste fudge and adjust sweetness by adding additional liquid stevia, if desired.
- Prepare a 9"x4" loaf pan by lining it with parchment paper.
- Pour fudge into loaf pan and place in freezer for about 15, until just set.
- Remove fudge and cut into 1" x 1" pieces. Store in an airtight container in the fridge or freezer.

Serves: 12

Serving Size: (2) 1" pieces

Calories: 172

Fat: 19.6 grams

Raspberry & Coconut Fat Bombs

INGREDIENTS

1/2 cup coconut butter

1/2 cup coconut oil

1/2 cup freeze dried raspberries

1/2 cup unsweetened shredded coconut

1/4 powdered sugar substitute such as Swerve or Truvia

Instructions:

- Line an 8"x8" pan with parchment paper.

- In a food processor, coffee grinder, or blender, pulse the dried raspberries into a fine powder.

- In a saucepan over medium heat, combine the coconut butter, coconut oil, coconut, and sweetener. Stir until melted and well combined.

- Remove pan from heat and stir in raspberry powder.

- Pour mixture into pan and refrigerate or freeze for several hours, or overnight.

- Cut into 12 pieces and serve!

Serves: 12

Serving Size: 1 piece

Calories: 234

Fat: 23.6 grams

Strawberry Cheesecake Ice Cream Cups

INGREDIENTS

1/2 strawberries, fresh or frozen, mashed well

3/4 cup cream cheese, softened

1/4 cup coconut oil, softened

10-15 drops liquid stevia

1 teaspoon vanilla extract

Instructions:

- Combine all ingredients in a medium sized bowl and mix with a hand mixer until smooth and creamy. Can also be done in a food processor or high speed blender.)

- Spoon the mixture into mini muffin silicon molds or small candy molds. Place in the freezer for about 2 hours or until set.

- When done, unmold the fat bombs and place into a container. Keep in the freezer and enjoy any time!

Serves: 12

Serving Size: 1 bite

Calories: 67

Fat: 7.4 grams

Peppermint Pattics

INGREDIENTS

¾ cup melted coconut butter

¼ cup finely shredded, unsweetened coconut

2 tablespoons cacao powder

3 tablespoons coconut oil, melted

½ teaspoon pure peppermint extract

Instructions:

- Mix together melted coconut butter, shredded coconut, 1 tablespoon of coconut oil and peppermint extract

- Pour coconut butter mixture into mini muffin tins that have been lined with paper liners. Fill half way.

- Place in refrigerator and allow to harden for about 15 minutes.

- Mix together 2 tablespoons coconut oil and cacao powder.

- Remove muffin tin from refrigerator and top each one with chocolate mixture.

- Return to refrigerator until the chocolate has set.

- When ready to eat, simply set the peppermint patty cups on the counter for about 5 minutes and unmold from muffin tin.

Serves: 12

Serving Size: 2 pieces

Calories: 80

Fat: 7 grams

Buttery Pecan Delights

INGREDIENTS

8 pecan halves

1 tablespoon unsalted butter, softened

2 ounces neufchâtel cheese

1 teaspoon orange zest, finely grated

pinch of sea salt

Instructions:

- Toast the pecans at 350 degrees fahrenheit for 5-10 minutes, check often to prevent burning.
- Mix the butter, neufchâtel cheese, and orange zest until smooth and creamy.
- Spread the butter mixture between the cooled pecan halves and sandwich together.
- Sprinkle with sea salt and enjoy!

Serves: 2

Serving Size: 2 pecan sandwiches

Calories: 163

Fat: 16 grams

Fudge Oh So Chocolate

INGREDIENTS

1 cup coconut oil, softened

1/4 cup coconut milk (full fat, from a can)

1/2 teaspoon sea salt

1-3 drops liquid stevia

1/4 cup cocoa powder

1 teaspoon vanilla extract

Instructions:

- With a hand mixer or stand mixer, whip the softened coconut oil and coconut milk together until smooth and glossy. About 6 minutes on high.
- Add the cocoa powder, vanilla extract, sea salt, and one drop of liquid stevia to the bowl and mix on low until combined. Increase speed once everything is combined and mix for one minute. Taste fudge and adjust sweetness by adding additional liquid stevia, if desired.
- Prepare a 9"x4" loaf pan by lining it with parchment paper.
- Pour fudge into loaf pan and place in freezer for about 15, until just set.
- Remove fudge and cut into 1" x 1" pieces. Store in an airtight container in the fridge or freezer.

Serves: 12

Serving Size: (2) 1" pieces

Calories: 172

Fat: 19.6 grams

Cinna-Bun Balls

INGREDIENTS

1 cup coconut butter

1 teaspoon vanilla extract

1 cup full fat coconut milk (from a can)

1 cup unsweetened coconut shreds

1/2 teaspoon cinnamon

1/2 teaspoon nutmeg

1 teaspoon sugar substitute such as Splenda

Instructions:

- Combine all ingredients except the shredded coconut together in double boiler or a bowl set over a pan of simmering water. Stir until everything is melted and combined.
- Remove bowl from heat and place in the fridge until the mixture has firmed up and can be rolled into balls.
- Form the mixture into 1" balls, a small cookie scoop is helpful for doing this.
- Roll each ball in the shredded coconut until well coated.
- Serve and enjoy! Store in the fridge.

Serves: 10

Serving Size: 1 ball

Calories: 273

Fat: 30.9 grams

Vanilla Mousse Cups

INGREDIENTS

8 ounces (1 block) cream cheese, softened

1/2 cup sugar substitute such as Swerve or Truvia (Stevia)

1 1/2 teaspoons vanilla extract

dash of sea salt

1/2 cup heavy whipping cream

Instructions:

- Add the first four ingredients to a food processor or blender.

- Blend until combined.

- With blender running, slowly add the heavy cream.

- Continue to blend until thickened, about 1-2 minutes. Consistency should be mousse like.

- Prepare a cupcake or muffin tin with 6 paper liners and portion the mixture into the cups.

- Chill in the fridge until set and enjoy!

Serves: 6

Serving Size: 1 piece

Calories: 199

Fat: 20.2 grams

Rich & Creamy Fat Bomb Ice Cream

INGREDIENTS

4 whole pastured eggs

4 yolks from pastured eggs

⅓ cup melted cocoa butter

⅓ cup melted coconut oil

15-20 drops liquid stevia

⅓ cup cocoa powder

¼ cup MCT oil

2 teaspoons pure vanilla extract

8-10 ice cubes

Instructions:

- Add all ingredients but the ice cubes into the jug of your high speed blender. Blend on high for 2 minutes, until creamy.
- While the blender is running, remove the top portion of the lid and drop in 1 ice cube at a time, allowing the blender to run about 10 seconds between each ice cube.
- Once all of the ice has been added, pour the cold mixture into a 9×5" loaf pan and place in the freezer. Set the timer for 30 minutes before taking out to stir. Repeat this process for for 2-3 hours, until desired consistency is met.
- Serve immediately. Top with chopped nuts or shaved dark chocolate, if desired.
- Store covered in the freezer for up to a week.

Serves: 5. Serving Size: 1 cup
Calories: 431
Fat: 44.3

English Toffee Treats

INGREDIENTS

1 cup coconut oil

2 tablespoons butter

1/2 block cream cheese, softened

3/4 tablespoons cocoa powder

1/2 cup creamy, natural peanut butter

3 tablespoons Davinci Gourmet Sugar Free English Toffee Syrup

Instructions:

- Combine all ingredients in a saucepan over medium heat.
- Stir until everything is smooth, melted, and combined.
- Pour mixture into small candy molds or mini muffin tins lined with paper liners.
- Freeze or refrigerate until set and enjoy!
- Store in an airtight container in the fridge.

Serves: 24

Serving Size: 1 piece

Calories: 142

Fat: 15 grams

Fudgy Peanut Butter Squares

INGREDIENTS

1 cup all natural creamy peanut butter

1 cup coconut oil

1/4 cup unsweetened vanilla almond milk

a pinch of coarse sea salt

1 teaspoon vanilla extract

2 teaspoons liquid stevia (optional)

Instructions:

- In a microwave safe bowl, soften the peanut butter and coconut oil together. (About 1 minute on med-low heat.)

- Combine the softened peanut butter and coconut oil with the remaining ingredients into a blender or food processor.

- Blend until thoroughly combined.

- Pour into a 9X4" loaf pan that has been lined with parchment paper.

- Refrigerate until set. About 2 hours.

- Enjoy!

Serves: 12

Serving Size: (2) 1" pieces

Calories: 287

Fat: 29.7

Conclusion

Thank you again for downloading this book!

I hope this book was able to inspire you to get into the kitchen and whip up some delectable, low carb, high fat desserts!

When you make these recipes, please share them with your friends and family, let them know about the book, and encourage them not to be intimidated by low carb, high fat foods.

Finally, if you enjoyed this book, please take the time to share your thoughts and post a review on Amazon. It's greatly appreciated!

Thank you and bon appétit!

61297037R00056

Made in the USA
Middletown, DE
18 August 2019